MW01109667

Expect good!
Rhonda

Presented to

_____

From

_____

Date

_____

Message

_____

_____

THE EMERGE SUCCESSFULLY SERIES

Keys to

Answered Prayer

RHONDA SCIORTINO

Unless otherwise noted, Scripture quotations are taken from the *Holy Bible: New International Version® (NIV).* Copyright © 1973, 1978, 1984 by Zondervan Publishing House, Grand Rapids, Michigan. Used by permission.

Scripture quotations marked NKJV are taken from the *Holy Bible, New King James Version®.* Copyright © 1982 by Thomas Nelson, Inc. Used by permission. All rights reserved.

Scripture quotations marked NLT are taken from *The Holy Bible: New Living Translation,* copyright © 1996. Used by permission of Tyndale House Publishers, Inc., Wheaton, Illinois. All rights reserved.

Scripture quotations marked MSG are taken from *The Message.* Copyright © by Eugene H. Peterson, 2000, 2001. Used by permission of NavPress Publishing Group.

First Printing: November 2012
ISBN: 978-0-9830921-7-9
Library of Congress Control Number: 2011917325

Published by:
N&SMG, Inc.
P.O. Box 13175
Newport Beach, CA 92658
Printed in the United States of America

CONTENTS

DEDICATION

*This book is dedicated
to everyone who ever prayed
and received no answer.*

"Ask, and it will be given to you;
seek and you will find; knock and
the door will be opened to you."

—Jesus, as recorded in the *Holy Bible*,
Book of Matthew,
Chapter Seven, Verse Seven

INTRODUCTION

In writing these "keys" to answered prayer, one might assume that I believe this to be an all-inclusive list and all you will ever need to know about getting your prayers answered. The truth is that the more I learn about God and His Word, the more I realize I yet have to learn.

These keys are not intended to be the final word on answered prayer. Neither is this intended to be

Prayer doesn't always result in the specific answers we would like to have; in fact, sometimes the answer appears to be very different from what we had hoped for. Yet other times the results are better than what we can ask or imagine! But in every case, prayer connects us with God. When we connect with God through prayer, we tap into His guidance, peace, and wisdom.

Only God knows what stands between you and the answer you seek.

There is a God, and He has given each of us a "Life Assignment." In fact, we've been created specifically for fulfillment of our own unique Assignment. In Ephesians 2:10 we read, "For we are God's handiwork, created in Christ Jesus to do good works, which God prepared in advance for us to do."

Our Life Assignments are dramatically different, and no one else is quite able to accomplish what we have been designed to do. So, how do we determine our Assignment? You guessed it! We do it through prayer. Prayer connects us with our Creator—the One who created us and the work we were specifically designed to accomplish.

Our life experiences are the foundation of our Life Assignments. Regardless of how difficult or downright ugly they were, they prepare and equip us for our Assignments. For example, I was abandoned by my parents and raised by maternal grandparents. They were verbally and physically abusive atheists who tried to teach me that there was no God. For a brief time, I was placed in the care of a wonderful Christian family who introduced me to Jesus. Although I was placed back in the care of my abusive grandparents until I emancipated at sixteen, that foster family introduced me to Jesus and taught me how to connect to Him through prayer.

For all the years that I was in that abusive childhood environment with my grandparents after meeting Jesus, I prayed for my grandparents to stop hurting each other and me. I prayed that my mother or father would come get me. None of those prayers were answered in the way that I expected. I hung onto my faith that there was a God, but I drew the conclusion that He created the solar system, the laws that govern it and the people; and then He stepped back for us to take it from there. I didn't know it then, but I've since heard that this belief system is referred to as the "clockmaker God."

When I was fourteen, I met a teacher who inspired me to seek God in a church. I got a ride to a church, and I asked to be baptized. I didn't understand it then, but looking back I can see clearly that I wanted to belong, to be a part of something bigger than myself.

That particular church denomination had a standing rule that one must complete a year of classes before being baptized. So I signed up for classes, found rides every week, and was approved for baptism at the age of fifteen. By the time I completed those classes, I had grown from believing that God created the world, set it in motion, and then stepped back—unable or unwilling to step in to help—to concluding that God "helps those who help themselves." Back then, my understanding of God's involvement in our lives hinged on our works.

Through the years of believing that God existed and was somewhere, but still not relying on Him for anything, I thought that God had an elusive set of rules that changed frequently. Even worse, I thought those rules were always slightly beyond my understanding. Although I read the Bible in prescribed daily readings, I viewed the contents as a mixture of history and metaphor that had little to do with me. Until one day.

I was on the fifth day of a migraine headache when my boss did what he called "laying hands on me." He prayed as I had never heard anyone pray and quoted Scriptures that I couldn't remember ever hearing.

My boss made it sound as though those Scriptures that had been written to someone over two thousand years ago were meant specifically for me! When he stopped praying, the headache was gone, and amazingly, after nineteen years of wearing glasses or contacts, I no longer needed corrective lenses to see!

I had tangible evidence that God can and does intervene in our lives.

That experience changed my life in many ways. In addition to the obvious benefits of the excruciating pain being gone and of no longer needing glasses to see the alarm clock in the morning, I had tangible evidence that God can and does intervene in our lives in meaningful, measurable ways. My entire belief system was turned upside down. Yet, the questions of why He hadn't stopped the abuse of my childhood remained in my mind.

From that day many years ago to this, I have hungrily studied God's Word to try to figure out why some prayers get answered and some do not. Why some people experience a lifetime of unbearable heartache and others live in tremendous blessing.

People who enjoy a life of blessings know that there may still be challenges or hardships to face. But you can be assured that with each challenge or adversity, there is an innate opportunity to pray our way

through to a greater depth of faith.
Once we have prayed and received
the answer to our prayers, the result-
ing faith is something that can never
be taken away from us.

While the keys that follow are
not a formula, they are indicators of
conditions for our participation that
may play a role in the answers God
desires to provide. Because God
places such a high value on our individual free will, we bear some responsibility in receiving answers to
our prayers. For example, faith in
God is our choice. Faith in God's
ability to answer and His willingness
to do so is also our choice. Faith is

active, not passive, and it is far more powerful than is often assumed.

Experiencing God's blessings of love, wisdom, discernment, peace, health, joy, long life, financial prosperity, and all the other evidences of God's involvement in our lives requires our active participation. God will never force Himself on us. The requisite conditions always involve some level of faith and willingness on our part to cooperate with God in His plan for our lives.

Even among faithful Christians, some people get answers to prayer while others seem to suffer long and hard. Why? The answer lies in the clues to answered prayer as found in God's Word. There are at least twelve of these clues mentioned in the Bible that I call "keys," any one of which may open the doors to the results you want to see in your life or the lives of those you love.

I'm writing this to you now because I wish that someone had helped me understand all of these things back when I didn't know the first thing about prayer. As a teenager who was so eager to be baptized and accepted into the church, I was afraid to ask whether I should be praying to God, to Jesus, or to the Holy Spirit, or whether I should pray for the same thing day after day when I didn't see an answer, or whether I should ask for forgiveness for the same sin over and over again after feeling no sense of having been forgiven.

I pray these keys are helpful in unlocking the doors to answered prayer in your life. I pray that all who read and act on these keys receive blessings beyond measure. I pray that these keys unlock the doors that have kept you from living the life you were created to live so that you can fulfill God's good plan to which you were perfectly matched. I pray that you receive the full measure of blessings from the God who delights in the prosperity of His servants and who longs to give you the desires of your heart.

Key #1

Be Sure to Pray

Key #1

Be Sure to Pray

God's Word says, "You do not have, because you do not ask God" (James 4:2). So the first key is to *pray*. Prayer changes things. There are myriad reasons why people don't pray. Some don't think it will do much good. They have prayed before, saw no tangible results, and never tried again. Or they think that they have to be on their knees in church to pray. Or they think it has been so long since they spoke to God or they have done too much wrong, so He won't listen or answer even if they did pray. Or they plan to pray when they come up for air from a crazy, busy schedule, but they simply never find the time.

Rather than waiting to be in a specific building, in a certain posture, and at some specified time, say a silent prayer right where you are. You don't even have to stop what you are doing. Pray while you're doing what you're doing. A prayer while you are driving is better than no prayer at all! Talk to Jesus as you would talk to your best friend.

Pray while you're doing
what you're doing.

This is not to suggest that you shouldn't have a specific time and place where you go single-mindedly before God's throne of grace. By all means do that. But many are in a hectic season of life where they are running from the moment their feet hit the floor in the morning until they collapse into bed at night, so they put prayer off until they can get around to it.

Some people don't pray because they have a vague sense of not deserving the good that God desires to give them. If we have accepted Christ, we become new creatures in Him. The Bible tells us that when we receive Christ into our hearts, the "old us" passes away and a new spirit is born inside of us (2 Cor. 5:17). If we "feed" our new spirit on God's Word, it grows every day until one day we, and everyone else around us, realize that we are not who we used to be. We truly are new people.

From the moment we accept Christ, God sees us as new people

through the prism that is Christ. In other words, when we accept Christ, we are given His name, "Christian." We become entitled to all that Jesus earned for us. We are heirs of His promises. When a Christian comes to God in prayer in the name of Jesus, God hears and answers the same as He would for Jesus! So recognize that although the "old you" does not deserve the good that God wants to give you, He wants to bless you for Jesus' sake!

Some people don't pray because they don't truly believe that God will answer. Almost everyone has had the experience of praying for something that didn't happen. We have prayed for someone to be healed, yet that person died anyway. We have prayed for a job that was given to someone else or for a house that didn't work out. Many people experience unanswered prayer and quit praying altogether. Some conclude that God had a different plan. Some conclude that the thing they were praying for wasn't God's will. Sadly, some people draw the conclusion that there is no God.

The truth is that none of us ever truly know God's thoughts and plans because they are higher than our ability to comprehend. There is a spirit realm that we cannot see. If we could, I suspect that we would see spiritual warfare with the forces of evil trying everything within its power to discourage us and convince us that prayer is futile.

There is a spirit realm
that we cannot see.

If we could see the unseen, we would also see the spiritual battle that is taking place with God's army of angels dispatched by prayer and held in place by faith by prayer warriors who understand that there is so much more to this life than what we can see with our natural eyes.

Jesus said, "Keep on asking, and you will receive what you ask for" (Matt. 7:7 NLT), and we surely should do this. But when we keep on asking, it's not because God didn't hear us the first time, and it's not that we have to persuade Him to be good to us. He hears our every faith-filled prayer and He looks for people He can bless (2 Chron. 16:9). Yes, we should ask and keep on asking so that the enemy who does not want you to have all of God's blessings will retreat. When we lose faith or quit praying, we turn loose of what we've grabbed hold of in faith.

We know that each of us starts his or her journey in Christ with a measure of faith (Romans 12:3). It is up to us to exercise our faith and to grow it to the strength necessary for the fulfillment of God's plans for our lives. How? We build our faith by answered prayer.

The older we get, and the more answers to prayer we receive, the stronger our faith becomes. Once we have seen amazing, inexplicable answers to prayers, our faith will have matured so that we can believe for greater and greater miracles. The growth and maturity of faith is somewhat like expanding your mind through the acquisition of knowledge and wisdom. Once acquired, no one can ever take it away from you. So pray.

Key #2

Have Proper Motives

Key #2

Have Proper Motives

In James 4:3, God's Word says that prayer goes unanswered because we ask with wrong, selfish motives. God isn't an ATM machine that will, with the right password, spit out fame, fortune, or happiness. In fact, requests that are rooted in selfish, self-centered desires are a waste of time.

Take an honest assessment of your personal motives. Are you praying for something that will bring you fortune or fame, or that you think will make you happy? Or are you asking for help for others? Are you asking for something that will bring love, peace, joy, patience, health, good relationships, and all the other blessings that God desires for you? Or are you asking for something that could be in opposition to God's plan for your life? Or could you be asking for something that is less than what God has planned for you?

Make sure you're not asking for something that will hurt someone else. We should never waste valuable conversation with the Creator of the Universe by asking for something that will bring good to us at someone else's expense.

Consider your time with God the same way you would if you were granted a private meeting with the governor of your state. Imagine that the governor has agreed to hear you out and is likely to give you what you ask for, so long as it brings no harm to any other citizen. In fact, the likelihood of your request being granted increases as the numbers of others who will benefit grows. So, there is no reason to ask for something that would harm anyone else.

God has the ability and desire to bless you with the desires of your heart without harming anyone else in the process (Psalm 37:4). So asking for something that is based on a self-ish motive is unnecessary. God can move even unbelievers to work on your behalf, as evidenced by the story of the unbelieving magistrates of the Roman government ordering the release of Paul and Silas from prison (Acts 16:36).

Sometimes we pray with wrong motives, thinking that the end justi-fies the means. This notion of illegal or immoral actions being justified by

42

a good outcome often is the result of the inability to imagine how God can answer our prayers to resolve a seemingly impossible or highly complicated situation. But He can! In fact, He could answer the prayers of every Christian on earth all at one time without creating a power shortage in Heaven!

Sometimes we pray with wrong motives, thinking the end justifies the means.

God says in His Word to seek Him. Jesus said to seek first the kingdom of God and all the things we need will be given to us (Matthew

43

6:33). If we take this advice and set aside our own selfish motives to seek first and foremost His Kingdom, which Scripture says is righteousness (right living) and peace and joy in the Holy Spirit (Romans 14:17), then we'll automatically avoid praying with wrong, selfish motives. When we seek God's will, which is His good and perfect plan for our lives (Jer. 29:11), we'll run right into the wonderful life God has for us!

Key #3

Clean Your Heart

Key #3

Clean Your Heart

Do not pray with anger, hatred, bitterness, resentment, unconfessed sin, unforgiveness, an unrepentant heart, or guilt in your heart. Psalm 66:18 says, "If I regard iniquity in my heart, the Lord will not hear." Before you pray, confess your sins, repent, and forgive those who have sinned against you. Repent means "to turn away from." So, while it's good to confess your sins, it's important to ask God to help you to avoid sin in the future.

Jesus said in Mark 11:25 that if you hold anything against anyone, go work it out and forgive him or her, and then come back to God to pray. Forgive others who harm you regardless of how heinous the sin against you—especially if they don't deserve to be forgiven. This is critical to your well-being and to receiving the answers to your prayers.

If the people who hurt you are no longer in your life, then simply resolve the issue in your heart and mind. Forgive them and move on. Resolve not to think or talk about these people or what they did to you.

Many people are unwilling to forgive because they see forgiveness as letting the other person off the hook for the wrong he or she has done. But make no mistake about this important principle: Forgiveness benefits you more than it does the other person.

Forgiveness may be easier if you consider that in holding something against someone, you are making a judgment about that person. When we hold on to offense, we're judging the person's intent and believing that he or she intended to harm us. In many cases, the other person may not have intended harm to us at all, but was focused on his or her wants and needs without thought for the impact on anyone else.

Selfish, self-centered behavior is wrong; but even in the case of heinous intentional acts against us, it is an egotistical error of enormous proportion to think that any of us is qualified to judge any other human. We rarely know the thoughts and intentions of another, or all the facts involved. We don't know all of the extenuating circumstances. You are far better off to trust the burden of judgment to God and allow Him to handle what only He is qualified to handle.

Forgiving others is critical to receiving answers to your prayers.

In God's Word we learn that we reap what we sow (Gal. 6:7-8). In other words, God created the system that many call Karma—what goes around comes back around, according to the familiar idiom. So when you release bitterness, anger, and resentment toward another person and put the whole situation in God's hands, don't automatically assume that God will wipe away any consequences that the person has triggered in his or her life.

The truth is that while God does forgive a truly repentant person, He typically does not waive earthly consequences. For example, people who commit murder may accept Christ while in prison and be assured of eternal salvation, but they may still live the rest of their earthly days in prison paying the consequences for the crime of murder.

The Word of God says, "There is no condemnation for those who are in Christ Jesus" (Romans 8:1). If any unconfessed sin—including bitterness, anger, resentment, and unforgiveness (yes, holding on to offense is sin)—has kept you from approaching God and receiving all He has for you, talk to Him. Get it off your chest. God is ready and willing to forgive you. There's no valid reason to hang on to these negative feelings. God the Father already knows what you have done, and He knows what's in your heart. There's nothing you have done that He hasn't seen already! There's no sin that Jesus hasn't already paid for.

So don't hesitate; tell God you're sorry for the sinful deeds you did and the ugly emotions you're hanging onto. The instant you confess your sins, He forgives you. Now it's your turn to receive His mercy. Don't ask for forgiveness again for this particular sin. It's forgiven. God takes your sin and removes it "as far as the east is from the west" (Psalm 103:12). Imagine taking a cup of water and throwing it into the ocean. You cannot go back and retrieve that cup of water. It's gone. Absorbed forever. That's what God does with your sin. Once you've asked for forgiveness, let your guilt go.

You may feel totally justified in the ugly emotions you feel about the people who have hurt you or someone you love. But consider that our hearts are the "pipelines" through which God's blessings flow. When our hearts are clogged with ugly emotions, we have allowed the flow of blessings to be blocked. Holding on to the hurt, and the emotions that go along with the hurt, will hinder or block entirely the answers to our prayers. Either we can have God's peace, love, wisdom, discernment, and answers to prayers or we can have anger, bitterness, resentment, and unforgiveness. But we cannot have both.

Some people have a difficult time repenting for a wrong behavior that

they enjoy or for an addiction because they can't imagine how they're
going to live the rest of their lives
without committing that sin again.
It's true that our hearts should be
right—in other words, we ought not
to repent of a sin that we intend to
commit again and again with the intention of coming back to ask for
more forgiveness later.

The truth is, though, that God's
mercy is new every day and endures
forever (Lamentations 3:22-23). He
knows our weaknesses and frailties.
He knows the hurts that cause us to
self-medicate, to seek love in the
wrong places, and to seek worth and

value by sacrificing what's truly important. God said that His mercies are new every morning because He knew we would need them! The good news is that He has the power to deliver us from addictions and from the power of evil that would try to keep us from His mercy and from His good plan for our lives.

There is no advantage to holding on to sin, guilt, and negative emotions.

So ask God for forgiveness, receive His mercy, and ask Him for His strength to keep you from sinning again. Failing to do this will block the flow of God's blessings to you. There is no advantage to holding on to sin, guilt, and negative emotions. The degree that our hearts are blocked by negative emotions affects the degree to which our prayers will be unanswered.

God is able and desirous of blessing us with all the desires of our hearts—in fact, He's the one who placed them there. Imagine that the way God gets His blessings to us is through the spiritual "pipeline" that runs in and out of our hearts. To hasten receipt of what we need and want, we must clean out the blockages in the pipeline. Just as you wouldn't put good, fresh food in a bowl full of moldy, disgusting food, before we can receive God's peace, wisdom, discernment, love, joy, and all the other blessings He desires for His children to have, we must clean out the ugliness.

Jesus said that He would send the Comforter, God's own Spirit, to help us. Galatians 5:21-23 tells us that the evidence that we have God's Spirit within us is the degree to which our lives exemplify the qualities of love, joy, peace, patience, kindness, goodness, faithfulness, gentleness, and self-control.

All the evidences of God's own

Spirit flow through the "pipeline" that is our heart. So, if we are acting in less than loving, joyful, peaceful, patient, kind, good, faithful, gentle, and controlled ways, it's a good sign that there's something blocking the pipeline to our heart. Clean out the pipeline, and you clear the way for answers to your prayers and for all the blessings God wants you to have.

Decide today to let go of anger, jealousy, bitterness, resentment, un-forgiveness, and every other kind of negative emotion. Be honest about the negative emotions you've felt and the way you've expressed those emotions in your thoughts, words, and actions. Decide today to change. Your life and the answers to your prayers are far more important than holding on to old, ugly emotions that will hold you back from the good life God desires for you to live.

Ask for God's help and His mercy will help to open the "release" valve of your heart so that any ugliness can drain out. After you've cleaned out the pipeline, pray again. In cleaning out your heart, you are making yourself "blessable." Expect to be blessed.

Key #4

Believe That
You Will Receive

Key #4

Believe That You Will Receive

The fourth key to answered prayer is to believe that your prayers will be answered. Jesus told us, "Whatever you ask for in prayer, believe that you have received it, and it will be yours" (Mark 11:24). This means that we are to eliminate doubt, which is easier said than done. How can we imagine, for example, good health when we're in the midst of a life-threatening illness or in so much pain we can hardly function? How can we believe that there's prosperity for us when we're unemployed, homeless, or hungry with no prospects of improving our situation? How can we envision a happy marriage when we're alone or miserable in a toxic relationship?

The answer is something that many people have known for years—visualize having what you have asked for. However, what some people overlook is God's involvement in the process. God created the universe and the ways in which it operates. When we seek to cooperate with the laws of the universe and the One who created the universe, we become connected with The Source of all goodness.

So, how do we become connected to The Source? By giving our lives to Christ. This is different from "believing in" God or even believing that Jesus Christ is the only Son of God who died for our sins.

I spent many years struggling through life, thinking that if anything good was going to happen, it was because I was going to make it happen. I finally realized that the step beyond "believing" was to give my

control and my will over to Christ.
Once I did that, I became truly connected to God and His good plan
for my life. Answers to my prayers
began to show up in my life, and my
circumstances began to change in
remarkable ways. But I'm getting
ahead of myself. Let me explain.

Jesus said that whatever we are
able to believe that we receive, we
can have. The key is to change the
channel in your mind the same way
you would change the channel on
your television. When you catch
yourself thinking the worst, train
your mind to think of the thing you
desire.

When you feel a pain, rather than allowing your imagination to conjure up pictures of some horrible diagnosis that the pain could represent, intentionally see yourself as totally healthy and pain free. Imagine yourself doing what the pain prevents you from doing. When you are experiencing financial trouble, rather than let your mind wander to the worst possible outcomes of the present problems, intentionally see yourself prospering. Imagine what you will do when the money you need is in your bank account.

This is not a hocus pocus action to bring about magical change. It's the advice of Jesus, the only Son of God. With this intentional optimism, what some have called "positivity," we are called to cooperate with God in His will and purpose for our lives.

God knows better than we do
what we need.

Even when we find ourselves in circumstances that we are completely powerless to change, we can choose to have a hope-filled, positive attitude. The amazing thing is that our positive attitude, combined with faith in God and hope for His good plan for our lives, is a combination

70

that allows God to work everything out for our good.

God knows what we want, and He knows the plans He has for us. He loves us too much to give us things that are not good for us or things, experiences, and people who will distract us from His plan. In our own free will, we are free to go after those things. But for those of us who desire to follow God, we must accept that God knows better than we do what we need for the fulfillment of His perfect plan for our lives.

Sometimes the things we think will make us happy are the very things that could destroy us. A simple example of this would be the desire to live in a certain house and praying about it for months to no avail. God may be keeping you from the biggest mistake of your life! He may have your dream job lined up, which would require you to live elsewhere. Or He may have a better house for you.

As an example, I always wanted to grow my insurance agency into an insurance company bearing the risks and reaping the rewards rather than simply selling an insurance policy. Twice I was able to negotiate a deal that would eventually result in my ownership of an insurance company. The first time I learned that the deal wasn't as it had appeared to be. The second time my partners were located in Tower Two of the World Trade Building in New York City on September 11, 2001.

My prayers for ownership of an insurance company were not answered. But if they had been, I would probably not have written my first book, and subsequently never have been given the opportunity to speak to people all over the United States about overcoming adversity and succeeding not just despite, but specifically because of what they've been through. There are so many wonderful people that I would never have met and so many relationships that would have never enriched my life. My life now is so much better than it was back then. So keep in mind that even though we have to be able to really see ourselves living in the reality of the answer to our prayer, there is a possibility that God has something even better for us.

We were created in God's image. When you think of yourself being created in the image of God, rather than thinking of physical attributes (having two eyes, two ears, and one nose and a mouth), think about God as the Creator of the Universe. Since He's the Creator, we are creators as well! We "create" businesses, games, inventions, symphonies, books, and everything else the mind of man can conceive. In fact, we're the only species on the planet whom God has imbued with the ability to imagine, speak of, and bring to reality new ideas. So use those gifts and imagine what you want.

This is what "believing that you receive" is all about—using your God-given imagination to envision yourself and your loved ones actually seeing, experiencing, and living the lives you are praying for. Your prayers may not become reality until you can truly see them answered in your mind's eye.

As you pray, imagine the way things will be when your prayer is answered.

Do not allow yourself to contemplate any alternative less than what you desire. As you pray, imagine the way things will be when (not if) your prayer is answered. When your mind begins to wander to thoughts of *what if it doesn't happen*, take those thoughts captive and give them over to God. This means that when you catch yourself thinking anything contrary to what you have prayed for, ask God to take that thought from you and intentionally replace it with a picture of your answered prayer.

For example, if you're praying for someone to be healed, imagine that person doing something they cannot do now. When you notice a thought of sickness or death coming to mind, stop, take hold of that thought, visualize handing it over to Jesus, and then picture the person completely restored and totally healthy.

Another example would be if you

are praying about losing weight. Ask God to help you picture yourself at the healthier weight you want to be. Get this picture so deeply engrained in your mind that you truly think of yourself at your desired weight. Once your self-image has shifted to the thinner, healthier you, your mind will cooperate with decisions that will help you reach and maintain your desired goal. Many people are able to lose weight but then fail to keep it off. It's because their mindset about their size never changed. But when God changes your mind first, your behaviors will line up and the change will become a reality and your healthy weight will be an integrated part of your self-image.

This goes for whatever you're praying for. If you are praying for healing, visualize yourself doing what illness, injury, or disease currently prevents you from doing. Believe that you will receive healing. If it's a good marriage you want, imagine a life that you desire to live with your spouse. If you are praying for your child to straighten out, imagine that child happy, healthy, and living a great life.

If, on the other hand, you vacillate between thoughts of good and thoughts of disaster, you are being what the Bible refers to as "double-minded." In James 1:6-8, God says "But when you ask, you must believe and not doubt, because the one who doubts is like a wave of the sea, blown and tossed by the wind. That person should not expect to receive anything from the Lord. Such a person is double-minded and unstable in all they do." (Paraphrased)

But when you ask in prayer,
you must believe and not doubt.

So once you have prayed, deliberately replace any thought that is other than the desired result with a picture in your mind of what life will be like after your prayer is answered.

For many years I have used my imagination in conjunction with my prayers. I know it's God who answers my prayers—not me or the power of my mind or my imagination. But I give God something to work with—my faith.

When I actively use my imagination to envision life with my prayers answered, I'm leaning on Him and believing His love toward me and His goodness in my life. I know that I do not have to beg Him to do good because He's The Source of all goodness. I don't have to coax Him to answer my prayers because He delights in giving me good things. And I certainly do not have to persuade Him to do His perfect will in my life because the fulfillment of His good plan is the reason I was born.

Through the years I have "cooperated with God" by "believing that I would receive." I envisioned myself as a successful business owner when I was still working on the floor of my condo (because I had no money for furniture or for an office). I envisioned myself living in a house on the beach when I was living in a tiny little apartment without even a refrigerator. I saw myself driving a convertible Mercedes while I was driving an old clunker that I had bought from a junkyard. When I was overweight, I pictured myself thirty-five pounds smaller.

What are you praying for?
Can you see it in your imagination?

When my husband had a life-threatening infection as a result of a surgery following an accident, and the doctors told me that he wouldn't survive, I pictured my husband and myself walking hand-in-hand on the beach when we are in our eighties. I kept that vision in the forefront of my mind night and day, and I told him about it often.

I did become a successful businesswoman, living in a home overlooking the ocean and driving the cars I envisioned. My prayers for my husband were answered too; he is completely healed. Praise God! And we walk on the beach hand-in-hand weekly and plan to continue to do so when we are in our eighties. So, what are you praying for? Can you see it in your imagination? Can you close your eyes and feel the way you would feel if you just learned that your prayer was answered?

If you cannot imagine your

prayers answered, find a quiet place where you can close your eyes and use the imagination God gave you to visualize the answers you seek. Keep doing this every day until the picture in your mind is vivid and real.

Key #5

Apply God's Word

Key #5

Apply God's Word

God said His Word never returns to Him unfulfilled (Isaiah 55:11). He also said that He dispatches angels to bring His Word to pass. (Psalm 103:19-21). When we speak God's Word, we are literally aligning our will with His. He wants to bring His Word to pass in the lives of His children. We don't have to persuade or beg Him to answer our prayers that are aligned with His Word. Our victories are trophies for Him! Just like our children's victories delight us and make us look good, our victories in life glorify our Father in Heaven. This fifth key is about agreeing with God's Word by applying it in our lives.

Faith should not be passive. Answered prayer does not just appear in our lives by default. Imagine that faith is a verb. Faith activated is applying God's Word to the situations in our lives that need correction. The beginning of applying faith in our lives is to believe that God is able and that He desires to bless us with the desires of our hearts (Psalm 37:4). When we take God's Word as our own, and believe that He wants what's best for us, we begin to believe that our prayers will be answered. It is our faith that releases God's power in our lives.

Faith activated is applying God's Word to our circumstances.

The way to do this is to find a Scripture that is aligned with what you want to see happen, and then speak those words aloud and in prayers. For example, when someone in your family isn't behaving well, say, "As for me and my household, we will serve the Lord" (Joshua 24:15). Be careful, though, when you grab a Scripture out of context. Ask the Holy Spirit for guidance, and He'll direct you to His Word that will change your life.

When sickness or other adversity tries to interfere with your life, speak the Lord's words declared to you, "No weapon formed against me will ever defeat me" (Isaiah 54:17 paraphrased). When something upsetting or disappointing happens, declare, "My God works all things together for me because I love Him and I'm called according to His purpose" (Romans 8:28 paraphrased).

God's Word wasn't written solely for the people referenced therein; it was written for all of us, no matter who we are or when we lived in history. The Bible says that God does not change (Mal. 3:6) and that "Jesus Christ is the same yesterday and today and forever" (Heb. 13:8). So, God's Word is just as relevant and powerful for us today as it was when it was originally written.

God's Word also says that God does not show any favoritism (Acts 10:34), which means He responds equally to the faith of each person. A person of great faith receives great results. A person of little faith receives little results.

It's tempting to point to the disparate circumstances and individual Life Assignments as proof that God does have favorites. But despite the evil that exists in the world and our own free will to make choices that are not the best for us, God does have a good plan for each of us. The plan of each individual may look very different, but one thing is constant: God makes love, peace, joy, wisdom, discernment, mercy, and so much more available to everyone who faithfully seeks and obeys Him.

Many Scriptures include a condition, so be prepared to be obedient to the condition. For example, Psalm 35:27 says that God delights in the prosperity of His servants. The condition here is that we serve God. We cannot do what we want to do, disregarding God's will and His good plan for our lives, and then expect God to delight in our prosperity.

Be prepared to fulfill the
condition written in Scripture.

For example, if God's plan is for you to be a social worker, but your plan is to be a musician, God is not going to clear the path to your success as a musician. This doesn't mean He doesn't love you or that you won't enjoy eternal life with Him in Heaven when you die. But it does mean that you're not going to fulfill God's good plan for your life and have all that He wants you to have that comes along with it.

The idea of repeating Scriptures from the Bible as prayer is not new. The best-known prayer in the history of Christianity, commonly referred to as "The Lord's Prayer," has been repeated daily by millions of people since Jesus spoke those words two thousand years ago. Scriptures fill our hymns and prayer books. When we speak God's Word, we are aligning ourselves with God's will.

So, find Scriptures in God's Word that support what you want to happen in your life and the lives of those you care about and apply those Scriptures to your life in a tangible way. Be prepared to fulfill the condition that is contained therein. Then speak the Scriptures in your prayers and declare them aloud over your life and expect good results.

Key #6

Eliminate Negative Language

Key #6

Eliminate Negative Language

Once you have repented, prayed, envisioned your desired outcome, aligned your thoughts and behaviors with God's Word, and spoken Scripture, don't contradict your prayer with negative language. If you speak negative, worry-filled words after you pray, you will "cancel out" your prayers. The words you speak after your prayer reflect the true depth of faith that accompanied your prayer.

An illustration of this would be a criminal defense lawyer who requests that the judge hearing the case dismiss charges on the grounds that the defendant is innocent. Then he turns to the person next to him or her and says in a voice loud enough for the judge to hear, "I can't imagine the judge letting this guy get away with what he's done. He's obviously guilty." That lawyer cannot expect to successfully get charges against his client dismissed.

In the same way, we cannot ask God to act on something and then clearly demonstrate our lack of faith in His desire or ability to make it happen for us. God rewards faith. There is no reward for doubt, worry, or anxiety. In fact, His Word says that everything that is not faith is actually sin (Rom. 14:23). So, eliminate the negative talk that demonstrates doubt and unbelief.

When circumstances around you are bad, get very quiet. Talk to God rather than friends or family. God is the only One who can do anything about the situation. We should not recount our challenges, feelings, and fears to every friend, neighbor, and co-worker who will listen.

This is not to say that we cannot enjoy the solace and comfort of others or the good counsel of a pastor or Christian counselor or therapist. God's Word says that we should "rejoice with those who rejoice, and mourn with those who mourn" (Romans 12:15), which tells me that He places people in our lives to comfort us during our lows and to celebrate with us during our highs.

There is no reward for doubt,

worry, or anxiety.

God knows there will be times in our lives when we are moved to tears. He knows about every tear we cry. But feeling the emotions and taking comfort from others does not give us license to speak aloud our fears. When we go beyond speaking of the facts of what is going on in our lives and begin to speculate about fears for the future, we turn our focus to the problems rather than to the One with the solutions.

If we are totally honest, much of the conversation we have about our problems is spoken to others to elicit sympathy. Think about it. If I call a girlfriend and tell her about the car breaking down, the kids behaving badly, and my back hurting, what does that really accomplish? Unless my girlfriend happens to be a mechanic, she can't fix the car. Unless she's a child psychologist, she really can't do anything about the kids. And unless she's a doctor, she probably can't relieve the pain in my back.

While it may feel good to get all that off my chest, what I've really done is make my girlfriend feel bad by burdening her with my problems or wasting her time. She may be too nice of a person to tell me so, but she may pull away from the relationship when she realizes that after every time she speaks to me, she feels down. And in the time it takes to tell her all of the bad things that are going on with me, I haven't listened to whatever might be going on in her life. I haven't added value to her life or made her feel better about what may be going on in her life.

Talk about how you
expect things to improve.

There is nothing wrong with calling a girlfriend and asking for a ride or for her to babysit the kids or for whatever other specific need you may have, but pay attention to your language and make sure that you're not canceling out your prayers by talking about all the things that are wrong in your life as though they are never going to change. Instead, talk about how you expect things to improve.

Positive, hopeful conversation is uplifting and inspiring to others. Listening and helping others in the midst of whatever is troubling you demonstrates that you trust that God is working on your behalf and that your prayers will be answered. So eliminate negative language after you pray.

Key #7

Stand in Faith

Key #7

Stand in Faith

Regardless of how long it takes, when you've done all else, wait expectantly for your prayers to be answered! God says in Lamentations 3:25, "The Lord is good to those who wait hopefully and expectantly for Him, to those who seek Him [inquire of and for Him and require Him by right of necessity and on the authority of God's Word.]" (AMP)

Choose faith between the time when you are saying a faith-filled prayer followed by a resounding "amen," which means "as it is and so it shall be," and the time that you actually see the resolution you've asked for in your prayer. This is where patience is developed. This is what God meant in His Word when He said, "But let patience have [its] perfect work" (James 1:4 NKJV).

The perfect work of patience *is* answered prayer! Of course, it's natural for worried thoughts to come to mind. Friends ask, "What are you going to do if your prayers aren't answered?" Others may think that you're irresponsible for not wringing your hands and pacing the floor with worry. But God rewards faith. Worry is rooted in fear, and Jesus said "fear not" more than any others two words.

So, when a worrisome or anxious thought comes to mind, take it captive, give it to Jesus (2 Cor. 10:5), and replace it with a picture in your mind of your answered prayer. This is what it means when God's Word says, "Cast all of your anxieties on Him because He cares for you" (1 Peter 5:7). These are not just empty words. This is solid advice that will save you from many sleepless nights and much heartache.

*Cast your cares on God
in the middle of adversity.*

God not only cares for you, but knows exactly what you need. Since He has the big picture of what we were designed to do within His perfect plan for us, He knows what we need to resolve the problems that face us now, as well as those we aren't even aware of yet. When we roll our cares over onto Him, we're essentially saying, "I acknowledge that I do not see the big picture, what I truly need or how to get it. I do not have all the answers, but I know that You do. And I trust that You love me enough to work everything out beautifully—not just satisfactorily, but amazingly!" Casting your cares on God right in the middle of adversity is the most faith-filled action we can take.

Many people think that if they lose sleep over their concern about a sick loved one, they are demonstrating love and care. The truth is that when we stay up all night worrying, we are really showing that we do not trust that there is a God, that He loves our loved one more than we do, or that He is able to effectively resolve the situation. I'm not suggesting that we not stay up all night to care for others. But staying at the bedside of people whom we love to show compassion and to ease their suffering, trusting that God is working in the situation, is very different from worrying ourselves sick.

God tells us, "All the days of the desponding *and* afflicted are made evil [by anxious thoughts and forebodings], but he who has a glad heart has a continual feast [regardless of circumstances] (Prov. 15:15 AMP). This means that anxious thoughts and forebodings of bad things in the

116

future are "what ifs" that are evil. They steal our happiness. While waiting for answers to prayer, we must be especially on guard to ward off these "what ifs."

We need to examine seemingly unanswered prayers in the light of these keys to answered prayers. It helps to take an honest look at what's happening after we have prayed. Could these circumstances be part of God's plan and purpose? Is there negative emotion blocking the flow of God's blessings? Is there some wrong behavior or motive that is inhibiting the desired outcome? Are we canceling out our prayers with negative words? Is there any unconfessed sin in our lives? Did we give up and quit waiting expectantly for our prayers to be answered?

When we remain hopeful,
our patience is built.

We need to be mindful of the fact that God doesn't change. He is always good, He is Love, and His mercies endure forever. So, if God seems distant, it's not because He has moved away from us. We are responsible to control our faith, attitude, words, and actions.

Sadly, when many people pray

and don't see the answer they asked for in the period of time they thought was reasonable, they conclude (wrongly) that there is no God or that God doesn't answer prayer. These folks fail to ask the right questions. What we should ask whenever our prayers go unanswered is, "God, please show me if there is something in me or someone else that is blocking Your plan and purpose in this situation. Please show me how to cooperate with making Your perfect plan a reality."

When prayers seem to go unanswered for an inordinate amount of time, we must hold on to our hope.

This can be especially difficult for the "go-getters" who want to make things happen. For some, the passivity of waiting feels irresponsible, as though they are doing nothing. But waiting faithfully for God can be some of the most spiritually powerful times of our lives.

When we remain hopeful, even in the face of adversity and seemingly unchanging circumstances, our patience is built. During times like this, remember things can change in one day. Circumstances can change with one phone call, one chance meeting, and one touch of God. Once our patience is developed, like matured faith, it can never be taken away. Never, never give up. The answer you are waiting for may be just around the next corner.

Key #8

Do Something
While You Wait

Key #8

Do Something While You Wait

While you're waiting for the answer to your prayer, be willing to do something. Sometimes God is waiting for us to do what we can before He will do what we cannot. Sometimes what we are expected to do is mundane, and at other times it is quite out of the ordinary. God may lead you to do something that makes little sense to you, such as offering help to someone who isn't asking for it or striking up a conversation with a complete stranger.

There are many Scriptures in the Bible that promise blessings from God that are conditioned on people doing something first. For example, Jesus said, "Anything is possible if a person believes" (Mark 9:23 NLT). Of course, the condition here is that one must genuinely believe that the subject of his or her request is within the realm of possibility. This is not to say that our power and intention alone will bring the answer to our prayer. But our willingness to act on

the leading of God's Holy Spirit allows us to actively participate in
God's work in our lives and the lives
of others.

A story in the Old Testament
perfectly illustrates a test of obedience that triggered a release of God's
power. In 1 Kings 5:1-14 we read
about Naaman, a prominent army
captain for the king of Syria, who
contracted leprosy. There was no
cure for the devastating flesh-eating
disease. Because it was highly conta-
gious, people who contracted it were
expected to leave their homes and
families and were exiled from their
communities.

Facing the loss of everything he held dear, and desperate to find a cure, Naaman made his way to the home of God's prophet, Elisha. When he arrived, Elisha wouldn't come out to meet him; instead, he sent a servant to tell Naaman to go dip himself seven times in the Jordan River. (1 Kings 5:1-10).

Whatever God leads you to do, do it.

Naaman stormed away angry. After all, he could have dipped himself in one of the two rivers that were near his home in Syria. Why would he, an important man, follow the advice of this prophet who wouldn't even give him the respect of walking out his front door? But then one of Naaman's servants convinced him to do as Elisha requested; he had nothing to lose in doing this easy thing. When Naaman took the advice of his faithful servant and followed the prophet's guidance, he was healed. The implication of this story is that if Naaman had not been willing to do the seemingly ridiculous or embarrassing thing, he would have suffered a leper's fate. (1 Kings 5:11-14)

For me, following the leading of the Holy Spirit meant leaving a good job and the salary and benefits that went along with it to open my own business. My decision to start over with nothing and no safety net made no sense to any of my friends. But I knew it was something I had to do. My willingness to act on my faith paid off with a successful business, clients who became dear friends, and work that combined my vocation of insurance with my avocation to help protect the people and organizations that help abused children.

So, after you've spoken to God, listen for His leading. He's a gentleman. He will not push His will on you. It is as though God whispers rather than bellows His commands.

To hear or sense His leadings, carve out some time to sit silently and ask if there is something He is waiting for you to do. You may feel a sudden urge to do something for someone or call someone you haven't spoken to in years. Be open to whatever ideas come to mind at this time. Don't dismiss anything as absurd. Be willing to do as Naaman did, going into the water seven times. Whatever God leads you to do, as irresponsible, irrelevant, or insignificant as it may seem, do it. Doing what God leads you to do shows that you are taking responsibility for your part and are willing to cooperate.

"Own" your responsibility in seeing your prayers answered by beginning today to do something that is good for you. For example, people who are unwilling to give up cigarettes, alcohol, sugar, and a high-fat diet, probably shouldn't expect to pray that God miraculously make them healthier without having to give up the unhealthy things. This is not to discourage people from praying about their health. But people in this situation would be much more likely to receive the answers to their prayers after praying for strength to give up the things that may be contributing to their health problems.

Regardless of your present situation, you can do something, such as drink more water. If you want to lose weight, begin today to commit to walking a specified number of steps every day or to leaving at least one bite of food on your plate.

Do something starting now
that is good for you.

There is an old African proverb that says, "When you pray, move your feet." All of us can do something right now to show God that we're willing to do our part to bring about our miracle. St. Ignatius of

Loyola expressed this beautifully when he said, "Pray as if it all depends upon God, for it does. But work as if it all depends upon us, for it does."

If you have no idea what to do to take a leap of faith, or if there is nothing that you know to do that will move you closer to answered prayer, ask God for guidance and determine now to do your best to live righteously.

In Isaiah 58:6-9 God is essentially saying that right living paves the way to answered prayer. This means simply that your faith-filled prayers to your Father who loves you will be answered when you deliberately treat people well and make right choices for your life—even when, especially when, you're going through a trial.

*Decide right now to do your best
to live righteously.*

Be careful not to confuse this with earning your salvation. This has nothing to do with God loving you or wanting you to spend eternity in Heaven. The point here is that God tells us over and over in Scripture the part we can play in improving our lives. It's summed up simply as treating people well and making right choices. This can be as simple as not demanding your own way and going along with what others want to do. It can be offering help to someone without them having to ask. It can be smiling when it is the last thing you feel like doing.

Living righteously doesn't have to cost a cent and often doesn't take any extra time out of your schedule. So while you wait for your prayers to be answered, live right by doing something good for someone.

Key #9

Thank God in Advance

Key #9

Thank God in Advance

Thank God in advance of the time that you actually see your answered prayers come to pass. Praise Him for the answered prayers that you can't yet see. This shows that we believe in Him and in His ability and desire to answer our prayers.

For example, imagine that you purchased a lottery ticket and then checked the paper the next day for the posted numbers. Imagine that to your surprise, all of your numbers were posted as the winner of a $10,000,000 jackpot! Most likely you would call all of your family and friends, one after the next, and excitedly announce that you had won the lottery! You might throw a party, go pick out a new car, call your realtor friend to begin searching for a new house, and consider how you will be able to help loved ones in need.

In other words, you would naturally begin thinking about all of the ways that your new-found wealth would change your life. All of this and you haven't even received a single dollar yet! Your announcement and plans are made based upon your faith that the funds are as good as yours since the numbers on your lottery ticket now match the numbers posted in the newspaper.

It's the same way with prayer. If we really believe that there is a God, and we believe that God is able to answer our prayers, and that God wants to answer our prayers, and that our prayers are not based on wrong, selfish motives, and so on, then of course we can believe that the answer, like the lottery money won but not yet received, is on its way. Answers that we know are on the way are cause for thanks to God.

———— ✦—O ————

Praise God for the answered prayers that you can't see yet.

We must praise God not only because it pleases Him, but also because it reminds us that God heard us and is making arrangements to bring the answer to our prayers at exactly the right time. His timing is always perfect (Eccles. 3:11). He is never late, but He isn't early either.

Receiving answers to our prayers when we're not yet mature enough to handle them could be devastating.

Imagine giving the keys to a brand new Ferrari to an eight-year-old. Doing that would be putting too much power and temptation in the hands of a child who is not prepared to handle it, and the result would likely be tragedy.

Jesus provided a wonderful example for us of praising before His prayer was answered. In John 11:41-42, we read the story of Jesus raising his recently deceased friend, Lazarus, from the grave.

While Lazarus was still dead and his family was mourning and weeping, *The Message* version of the Bible records Jesus saying to the people,

"Go ahead, take away the stone." Then to God He said, "Father, I'm grateful that you have listened to me. I know you always do listen, but on account of this crowd standing here I've spoken so that they might believe that you sent me." Jesus proceeded to call for Lazarus to come on out, and Lazarus did!

Jesus praised God before
His prayer was answered.

Notice that prior to talking to God about the situation, Jesus took action and had the stone rolled away. All of this seemed absurd to those around Him. Lazarus' sister pointed out that her brother's body would stink because he'd been dead for four days. But Jesus seemed to ignore this comment, and went right ahead and thanked God while the result He sought still seemed completely impossible.

Another example of praise prior to answered prayer is in Daniel 2:17-24 when Daniel thanks God in advance for helping him interpret a dream before God actually did it. The faith implied in the appreciation before the answered prayer actually connects you to God, who cares about your pain. Psalm 56:8 says,

"You keep track of all my sorrows. You have collected all my tears in your bottle. You have recorded each one in your book" (NLT).

God responds to the faith that is inextricably linked to heartfelt praise. In Colossians 4:2 it says, "Devote yourselves to prayer with an alert mind and a thankful heart" (NLT). The alert mind keeps us aware of ideas and prompts by God to take actions that will lead to answered prayer and the fulfillment of His good plan for our lives. The thankful heart demonstrates our faith in God's ability and willingness to answer our prayers.

In my case, I have thanked God in advance of receiving what I've asked for over the years, and time and again God has come through for me. The answers I've received haven't always looked as I've imagined—in many cases they are much better than I could have dreamed!

When we praise God through tears,
He honors our sacrifice.

Praise is a powerful thing, and every one of us can do it—regardless of physical, financial, or emotional limitations. God's Word says that He inhabits the praises of His people

(Psalm 22:3). But praising and thanking God in the midst of a crisis or immediately following a tragedy can be the most difficult thing in the world to do.

When we praise God through tears and gritted teeth, He honors our sacrifice (Heb. 13:15-16), gives us His peace that truly does exceed all human understanding (Phil. 4:7), and gives us beauty for the ashes (Isaiah 61:3) of our painful experiences. And in the process, He makes stepping stones out of the worst of our circumstances to lead us out of our pain and into a life that glorifies Him.

Key #10

Fast

Key #10

Fast

While waiting for the answers to your prayer, consider giving up something and replacing it with time spent talking and listening to God or praising Him. Giving up something is referred to as a "fast." Jesus modeled the ultimate fast during the forty days and forty nights He spent in the wilderness with neither food nor wa-

ter. During that time of abstinence
and testing, His faith and resolve
were strengthened because He lived
on God's Word.

I'm not suggesting that we go
that long without food and water,
but that we find a way to use this
valuable tool in our lives to clear the
clutter and chaotic thoughts from
our minds and hear clearly from
God about what He wants for us.

God is not desirous of anyone
jeopardizing his or her life by going
without something the body needs,
so if there are health challenges that
would prevent you from a complete
fast, consider fasting from one spe-

cific thing that you enjoy. The more you enjoy the thing, the more you'll be reminded of it and think about it. Every time you think about the thing or activity sacrificed, you will be reminded to talk to God. Replace the time you would have spent enjoying the thing you've given up with time spent in conversation with God.

The greater the sacrifice,
the more power there is in it.

You can fast from just about anything. The greater the sacrifice, the more power there is in it. Some examples are fasting from chocolate or some other food you enjoy, from alcohol, from eating meat, or from a favorite television show. Every time you think of the thing you are doing without and crave to have it, say a prayer.

For those who medicate their pain with food, alcohol, cigarettes, drugs, pornography, sex, or whatever else distracts them from the pain they feel, fasting from their source of distraction is especially powerful. Fasting for even a few minutes from the subject of addiction is an important step to taking back control. You cannot give yourself fully to God if part of you is owned by addiction.

Each time we choose to talk to God rather than succumb to temptation is a time we are telling God, "I'm going to trust You to help me rather than finding my solace elsewhere." God honors the faith and strength that it takes to shift our reliance from the thing that brings us momentary relief to the One who brings eternal joy.

I know people who have fasted from food one day every week for years. Others skip one meal on one day every week and instead spend the time they would have spent eating sitting alone with God. Some spend the first few days of every new year fasting and hearing from God for direction for the year. These people talk of never again doing without fasting in their lives because of the insights and guidance they've received from God that they believe they would not have heard had they not made that sacrifice.

In Mark 9:15-29 we read about a father who brought his son to the disciples of Jesus for healing. The boy exhibited inappropriate and dangerous behaviors. The disciples prayed, but nothing happened. The father then took the boy to Jesus. He prayed, and the evil spirit that was ruining the boy's life was cast out and the boy was healed.

When the disciples asked why they weren't able to do the same after having done many other healings in the name of Jesus, He replied that this miracle could only be done with prayer and fasting. This story demonstrates the importance of regular prayer and fasting so that we are prepared to bring the power of God to any situation that comes to our attention.

When crisis occurs, it typically provides no prior warning. In the midst of tragedy there is no time to quietly steal away and give ourselves to fasting and prayer. So to be ready for whatever comes our way, we have to be "prayed-up" and "fasted-up" ahead of time, which is a power-filled combination of disciplines.

Be "prayed-up" and "fasted-up" ahead of time.

Many people follow the example of Jesus and separate themselves from others for a time of fasting and prayer before a big decision. For example, prior to my wedding I fasted from everything except water for seven days. I wanted to be sure that I was focused solely on the sacred commitment I was about to make.

This time alone while fasting serves to quiet the chatter and clear the pathway for hearing the whispered leadings of the Holy Spirit.

Fasting is perhaps more important now than ever before because of the communications and messages flying at us from every angle every day. All of us are bombarded 24/7 with non-stop information from the television, Internet, email, phone, printed media, social networking and, of course, face-to-face communication.

The information overload is so common that many of us don't even stop to think about the significant increase in the number of messages and amount of information coming at us in a day. For example, in the 1970's a television commercial often consisted of only one person talking about one product. In the average thirty-second television ad of today, we are hit with seventy-two images per second. To put this into perspective, the human eye is said to be able to process ten to twelve separate images per second. When you consider all that comes at you in a day, you can begin to appreciate the benefit of quiet time without distraction.

One powerful example of fasting was shared by a friend whose adult son went missing. Her son had gone on a trip with some friends in the vast Southern California desert. After he had separated from his friends at a party, the friends thought he had left with a girl, so they didn't get worried until the next day when he didn't return or call anyone.

Fasting helps us to hear God's leading.

Finally, my friend was notified. From the moment that she got the call that her son was missing, she refused to eat or drink.

Authorities scanned the desert with ATV's and a helicopter for several days and still couldn't find my friend's son. The police announced that they presumed the man was dead and ended the search.

But my friend and her husband wouldn't leave the make-shift camp they had set up. She said that she couldn't live the rest of her life without the closure of finding him. So without all of the support and equipment from the authorities, my friend, her husband, her daughter, along with her daughter's boyfriend, searched on foot in the vast desert in 110+ degree temperatures.

On the fifth day my friend, still refusing food or water, grew too weak to continue. She lay at the campground asking God to please show her a sign to find her son's body so that she could properly lay him to rest and finally have some peace. Within an hour of that request, her husband saw a large bird circling over one area again and again. He went in the direction of the bird, and there he found his son. My friend and her husband were able to lay their son to rest.

Fasting brought about resolution.

Although this was a tragedy and it did not end in the way that they had hoped for, my friend believes with all her heart that it was her fasting that led to finding her son and finding peace to go on.

This story is a good example of the fact that Christians do not always receive the answer we hope for in prayer. Of course, my friend prayed fervently for her son to be found alive and well. But there is evil in this world. Jesus said that we have an enemy who came to kill, steal, and destroy (John 10:10).

We cannot control all the choices that the people in our lives make that may put them at risk. But we can pray for their protection and pray for God to send His people into their lives to speak to them about Jesus, His Kingdom, salvation, and His way of living. We can prepare to handle whatever arises by spending a regular time of fasting and prayer. And we may even be able to prevent tragedy by speaking into the lives of those we love, using the words God leads us to speak.

Whatever you may be praying for now, give something up at the same time. Every time you think of what you're missing during this fast, pray more fervently for the person or the circumstance that you have lifted up to God.

Key #11

Give to Others

Key 11

Give to Others

Give. When I mention this key to answered prayer, I'm often met with looks of frustration bordering on anger. People are often praying because they're in need of some material thing. They can't grasp why it's suggested that they give in the midst of their need. How are they supposed to give when they're broke?

I understand that the very nature of many prayers is that of a particular need. We need help and we are asking for it, so giving when we're the ones in need often makes no sense. But that is exactly when we need to give of our time and money because it demonstrates in a measurable way that we trust that God will meet our needs. God says in Malachi 3:10 that when we bring our whole tithe (a tenth of all we receive) into God's storehouse, then He will open the floodgates of Heaven and pour out a blessing larger than we can grasp.

Yes, I am suggesting that you

tithe of your time and your money, but please don't get hung up on the word "tithe" or a percentage of giving lest you miss the point.

The importance of giving cannot be underestimated. It's not so much that God wants your money as He wants your faith and trust. It requires faith to hand over your hard-earned money—the money you need to take care of your family and do what you want to do. It takes faith to give away something that is valuable to you.

So, when we give to others our money or other valued things in our lives, we are literally showing God that we trust Him to take care of us and to meet our needs and, more importantly, that He can trust us. Once we have demonstrated that we can be trusted, He will give us opportunities that will generate more revenue.

God takes it as a personal favor when we give to others.

Giving of your time is equally important. This includes spending the first few moments of every day with God. This also means giving time to help others. Your service can be in an organized fashion, such as volunteering at a church or other service organization. God said in His Word that when we do something good for the least of His children, we've done it for Him (Matt. 25:40). Imagine that! God takes it as a personal favor when we do something for one of His children.

You can also give of your time in ways that are spontaneous, such as going out of your way to help a co-worker with something they're having trouble handling, letting another car merge into your lane during rush-hour traffic, or calling someone who is going through a rough time to encourage him or her.

Taking the time to help others when you don't expect anything in return—especially helping those who can do nothing to us or for us—is taking Christ out of the church and out into the world. In this way, we can participate with God in answering the prayers of others.

Helping others while we are in need of answered prayer shows God that we are not entirely focused on ourselves and our needs but on God and what He wants done on earth. Helping others shifts our focus off ourselves, at least for a time, and onto someone else. There is always someone who has it worse than we do. And helping someone else shows we have faith that God is working on our behalf.

In expressing (exercising) our faith, we are making our faith stronger.

According to Proverbs 21:13, "If a man shuts his ears to the cry of the poor, he too will cry out and not be answered." To put it simply, if we don't help others, God may not help us. The recurring theme of reaping what we sow appears in God's Word (Gal. 6:7-9). So, when we help others, we will receive help in our time of need.

Treating others well, especially when they don't deserve it, shows our love for God in a tangible way. God's Word says, "The only thing that counts is faith expressing itself through love" (Gal. 5:5-6), so in giving love to others, our faith literally works to bring about the answer to our prayers. In expressing our faith, we are exercising it. And as is the case with any muscle that is regularly exercised, our faith subsequently gets stronger.

It can be so challenging to treat unreasonable or difficult people well. After all, they don't deserve it. They haven't earned it. They often mistake kindness for weakness, which some- times leads to their bad behavior worsening instead of improving. Nevertheless, we are called by God to love them.

When God calls us to love others (John 13:34), He isn't saying that we have to trust difficult people. He isn't demanding that we spend all our time with toxic people or that we try to solve all their problems. He is asking us to show our trust in Him by treating people well. In fact, God effectively says that if we have the means to help others but we are all talk and no action, the love of God isn't in us (1 John 3:17-18).

Sometimes treating people well looks like what is commonly referred to as "tough love." Yes, we are supposed to be loving, patient, kind, humble, long-suffering, and forgiving; but we may also be called upon to hold people accountable, deliver strong messages, or do other things that others do not like.

If God wants to use us in an uncomfortable situation, He will give us the right words.

Just as a real friend will tell you when you have something stuck in your teeth, when your zipper is down, or when the back of your skirt is tucked up into your pantyhose, we are supposed to be real friends to the people in our lives and tell them the hard truth when necessary.

When we are in a position to deliver a difficult message to someone, God asks us to do it with love (Eph. 4:15). We aren't expected to resolve everything, but when we are led by God's Holy Spirit to say something to someone, we must be willing to deliver His message in a loving way and trust God with the rest—even when there's nothing in us that wants to use our valuable time on this difficult circumstance. Nevertheless, we should try to engage in a conversation of love—even though we might end up in conflict with this person. If God wants to use us in an uncomfortable situation, He will give us the right words at the right time, and He will prepare the heart of the other person to receive and process the words He gives us to say. Following His leading to know when to talk and what to say is critical.

Act on the leading of God's Spirit.

So, while you're waiting for the answer to your prayers, listen and act on the leading of God's Spirit about giving your time, money, advice, or other resources to help others. Doing what God leads you to do, despite what you may or may not feel like doing, is obedience to God. Our obedience is a sacrifice we make to Him, and doing what is pleasing to God is one reason we get what we ask for in prayer (1 John 3:21-22).

Disobedience won't necessarily cost you your eternal life, but it robs you of faith, confidence, and the boldness to approach God with your requests. Since we know that faith overcomes evil (1 John 5:4), when faith is diminished, evil can get in and kill, steal, or destroy you and

God's good plan for you.

Behaving in a loving way toward everyone, especially those who are difficult to love, is a tangible way of honoring God. And as we see in Deuteronomy 28 and throughout the book of Proverbs, God protects, blesses, and rewards those who honor and obey Him. So, show your faith by giving to others. And grow your faith by giving that which will be a personal sacrifice. Do it for God, and watch with delight what He does for you.

Key #12

Trust God

Key #12

Trust God

Trust God's ability to bring about miracles however He does it. Sometimes it's instantaneous and supernatural, but sometimes miracles come through the most natural, even mundane, circumstances or series of events. If you trust that God will resolve your impossible situation in your favor, then one way or another,

He will! Trust God's desire to do good things for you, but resist the temptation to tell Him how it ought to be done. God wants to bless and prosper you. He planted the deepest desires of your heart. He knows what they are.

Trust God's desire
to do good things for you.

The way to learn to trust God is the same way you would learn to trust any friend. If you have a friend who shows up in a timely manner every time he or she makes a plan with you, you know that if you invite your friend to come over Saturday at 6:30 p.m. for dinner, you had better have dinner cooking and the house ready because, barring any unforeseen incident or emergency, your friend will be there Saturday at 6:30! You wouldn't be unprepared and totally surprised to see your friend standing at the door then because your friend can be trusted to show up on the right day at the specified time.

In the same way, God wants to earn your trust. The way that happens is by knowing Him. The easiest way to get to know Him is by reading about Jesus in the first four books of the New Testament, the Gospels (this means "good news"): Matthew, Mark, Luke, and John. These four men wrote about Jesus from their personal experiences with Him.

Jesus is the Son of God, and everything He said and did was a perfect representation of God. He said and did only what God instructed him to say and do (John 12:50). So when we know Jesus, we gain a better understanding of God. When we have a better understanding of God—His love for us, His desire to protect us, to bless us, and to prosper us—then our confidence, trust, and boldness will increase.

For example, if you are suffering with pain from an accident or disease but you are reluctant to ask for healing, or if you have prayed but you haven't experienced any relief yet, consider that there is not one reference in the entire Bible where God refused to heal someone. To the contrary, Bible reference after Bible reference tells us that Jesus "healed them all" (Matt. 4:24, 8:16, 12:15, 15:30; Luke 4:38, 6:19). And since Jesus is the perfect representation of God, we know the will of God from His Word (John 14:6-11), and it is clearly His will to heal. So even when you see or feel no difference, pray and trust that He can, He wants to, and He will heal you.

*Trust God's in matters
of health and finances.*

If you are struggling with a lack of money and you aren't comfortable with asking God to provide for you, consider that He delights in our prosperity (Psalm 35:27), that He gives us ideas and inventions to help us succeed financially while helping others (Prov. 8:12), and that He has blessed and prospered many people, including Abraham and Lot (Genesis

12:5, 13:2-5), Isaac (Genesis 26:12), Jacob (Genesis 30:25), Laban (Genesis 30:27), Esau (Genesis 36:6), Boaz (Ruth 2:1), David (1 Chron. 22:14, and Solomon (2 Chron. 1:12).

Don't misunderstand the Scripture that talks about the lure of wealth as though wealth itself was a bad thing (Mark 4:18-20). Many people make the mistake of jumping to the conclusion that money itself is bad, and consequently they accept less than what God has for them. Wealth is God's idea, but it is to be used to help others. In other words, we are to use wealth to help people, and never to use people to gain wealth. It's all right to have wealth as long as it doesn't have you.

Wealth is only a tool and must never define who you are. In my case, it took an enormous amount of trust in God to leave a good job to start my own business. But by taking that leap of faith and sticking with it, God rewarded my efforts And with the wealth He provided, I have been able to bless others in ways I would never have been able to without it.

Just the same as we have to learn to trust God in matters of health and finances, if you are in need of help with a relationship, turn to God. He wants us to have peace and joy in our relationships (Matt. 10:13). He wants to bless people by bringing peace to chaotic situations (Matt. 5:9, Mark 9:50).

Hold on to God in the midst
of an environment of anger.

God's way is the way of peace (Luke 1:79), so when we follow the example of Jesus, we bring peace into difficult circumstances. This doesn't mean that there is no chaos or disharmony, but that we maintain our peace in the midst of it. By holding on to God and remaining peaceful in the midst of an environment of anger, we can influence the entire situation for good.

This also means that we don't turn a blind eye to wrongdoing just to keep peace. Feigned ignorance of wrongdoing isn't true peace. When we follow God's leading to do or say what He wants done or said, He will do what needs to be done to create true, lasting peace.

So regardless of the circumstances you face, trust God. If you have prayed and things seem to be no better or even appear to have worsened, trust that God is working on your behalf. Hold on to your faith. When you are in doubt, give

God the benefit of that doubt, trusting that He will come through at the perfect time. Trust that He will ultimately work together for good all things for you (not some things or only those things that make sense) because you are doing your best to love Him and respond to His call and fulfill His purpose for your life (Romans 8:28).

Conclusion

God can and does honor the simplest of prayers. He hears us and responds to us when we simply whisper the name of Jesus. A story about a missionary who introduced the gospel to a very primitive group of people illustrates this. When the missionary left the primitive tribe that he had tried to minister to, he didn't feel as though he could count his time there as a great success. Because of the language challenges, he had succeeded only in teaching them the Lord's Prayer; and even then, he wasn't sure they had any clue what they were saying or what it really meant.

Some years later the missionary returned to that mission field to find that the natives were joyful people who were prospering, thriving, and very faithful to the one true God and their worship of Him. When he heard them pray, he was shocked to hear their recitation of what they thought was the Lord's Prayer. What he'd taught had since been taught to the next generation, who had in turn taught it to their children. To the old missionary, the prayer sounded very different from what he'd taught them.

These people were repeating syllables they thought they'd heard—words they didn't know in a language they didn't understand. What they were saying were syllables of words that didn't exist. They surely didn't understand what they were saying. But despite the fact that their words weren't perfect, that they didn't pray in the "ideal" posture (whatever that may be), that they didn't include specificity of requests, and that they didn't pray with what some would consider an "acceptable level" of seriousness and intensity, God honored and prospered them.

So, pray, check your motives, ask for forgiveness, receive mercy, and forgive others. Refuse to give in to negativity, choose faith, be willing to do something, thank God in advance, and then imagine receiving the answers to your prayers. Give something up until you receive your answer. Be good and treat everyone with love. Believe in God's ability and His desire to give you the desires of your heart—trusting that He placed those deepest desires in your heart in the first place! And know that even if you don't do everything perfectly, God hears you and knows your heart.

By focusing on these key actions in your prayer life, you will see the goodness of God in the land of the living—that's here on earth, in your lifetime! May God bless you exceedingly, abundantly above and beyond all you can ask for, hope for, or imagine.

God's Desire for You

Here are paraphrases of some of the Scriptures that tell us that God wants to give us the desires of our hearts.

He delights in our prosperity.

Psalm 35:27

He has a good plan for your life.

Jeremiah 29:11

God wants us to prosper and be in good health even as our soul prospers.

3 John 2

In Heaven there is no sickness, poverty, pain, etc.

Revelation 21:4-7

Trust God and not your own judgment. If you let Him lead you, He will clear the road for you to follow. Proverbs 3:5-6

The prayer of faith restores the sick.
James 5:15

As much as we love our children and want to help them, God our Father loves us more! Matthew 7:11

He provides for us from His riches and glory in Christ Jesus. Philippians 4:19

If we seek first God's kingdom, all the things we want will be given to us.
Matthew 6:33

God generously provides for our enjoyment.
1 Timothy 6:17-18

The Word of God is at work in the lives of those who believe it. 1 Thessalonians 2:13

He never said no to anyone who asked for healing.

Matthew 4:24
Matthew 8:16
Matthew 12:15

About the Author

Rhonda Sciortino is what she calls a "fully yielded believer," meaning that she wants what God wants for her life. Abandoned at six months of age, Rhonda spent the first sixteen years of her life as a ward of the court. Most of those years were lived in a filthy, dilapidated shack the size of a garage without working plumbing. Rhonda, like many other successful survivors, developed coping mechanisms that allowed her not only to survive abandonment, poverty, hunger, and severe abuse, but to succeed in business and in life specifically because of them.

Rhonda went from a shameful beginning to living an amazing life, and she considers it part of God's assignment for her life to help others to find and fulfill His beautiful plans for their lives. She lives in Southern California with her husband, Nick, near their daughter and her family.

Additional information is available at www.rhonda.org.